Science Fiction Pioneer

Jules Verne

Science Fiction Pioneer

A Story about Jules Verne

by Tom Streissguth
illustrations by Ralph L. Ramstad

A Creative Minds Biography

Carolrhoda Books, Inc./Minneapolis

Aux Rouffiac de France, la famille aux aventures diverses et étranges

Text copyright © 2001 by Tom Streissguth
Illustrations copyright © 2001 by Ralph L. Ramstad

This book is available in two editions:
Library binding by Carolrhoda Books, Inc.,
   a division of Lerner Publishing Group
Soft cover by First Avenue Editions,
   an imprint of Lerner Publishing Group
241 First Avenue North
Minneapolis, MN 55401 U.S.A.

Website address: www.lernerbooks.com

Library of Congress Cataloging-in-Publication Data

Streissguth, Thomas, 1958–
   Science fiction pioneer: a story about Jules Verne / by Tom Streissguth; illustrations by Ralph L. Ramstad.
      p.   cm. — (A Creative minds biography)
   Includes bibliographical references and index.
   Summary: Follows the life of the well-known novelist from his childhood in Nantes, France, to his career as a successful fiction writer whose imaginative works often gave glimpses into the future.
   ISBN 1-57505-440-X (lib. bdg. : alk. paper)
   ISBN 1-57505-623-2 (pbk. : alk. paper)
   1. Verne, Jules, 1828–1905—Juvenile literature. 2. Authors, French—19th century—Biography—Juvenile literature. [1. Verne, Jules, 1828–1905. 2. Authors, French.] I. Title. II. Series.
PQ2469.Z5S77   2001
843'.8—dc21   99–006824

Manufactured in the United States of America
2 3 4 5 6 7 – MA – 08 07 06 05 04 03

Table of Contents

1

Setting Sail

Jules Verne ran from his house down to the harbor of Nantes. He soon reached the wharves on the Loire River, the longest river in France. Ships of all sizes came here to unload their cargo, mostly sugar and spices from the Caribbean. At one end of the harbor, Jules spotted a big sailing ship lying at anchor. Carefully, as silently as he could, he walked up the gangplank, watching for a guard.

There were no guards on the ship to stop the mischief of an eight-year-old boy. Jules wandered the deck and imagined sailing to distant seas and continents. He could discover unknown islands, cross the wide Pacific, and meet islanders that no sailor or explorer had ever seen.

Jules walked to the back of the ship and passed through a low doorway to the officers' quarters. He saw the shipmasters' narrow bunks and their shiny brass instruments—sextons, compasses, telescopes. In the captain's cabin, he saw a small desk covered with writing paper and sailing charts. With these instruments and papers, and a good crew, Jules figured he could find his way anywhere in the world.

Jules climbed back to the top deck and entered the wheelhouse, the small cabin where the pilot steered the ship. Making sure that no one could see him, he grasped the wheel and gave it a turn.

Nothing happened. The ship was tied to the wharf. But in his imagination, Jules was sailing slowly out of the harbor. The wind was filling his sails, and he was steering the ship down the shallow Loire River and into the stormy Atlantic Ocean.

The people of Nantes had a saying: "As honest as Verne." They were speaking of Jules's father, Pierre Verne, who worked as a lawyer. Pierre's father had also been a lawyer and a judge as well. When Jules was born on February 8, 1828, the family was certain that another honest Verne had come into the world.

Pierre expected his first son to follow in his father's footsteps. He imagined Jules studying hard, staying in Nantes, and earning a living as a lawyer. Instead, young Jules was dreaming of traveling to exotic places and finding adventure on the high seas.

Jules lived with his family on Ile Feydeau, a small island in the Loire River. The wealthiest businessmen in Nantes had built their houses on Ile Feydeau. Pierre Verne wasn't wealthy, but he provided well for his wife, Sophie, and for his children: Jules, Paul, Anna, Mathilde, and Marie. He was dedicated to the law and spent many hours at home studying his law books and papers. Both Pierre and Sophie Verne went to church regularly. They taught their children to have a purpose in life and to work hard to reach their goals.

Pierre Verne was a strict father and a hard worker. But he also shared a love of poetry and music with his family. Under the light of oil lamps, the Vernes spent many long evenings together, reading poetry and listening to songs that Pierre Verne wrote.

From his father and friends, Jules also heard many stories of the sea and of distant countries. He learned about the latest explorations in Africa, Antarctica, and the Americas. There was even an explorer in the family. Jules's uncle had married the sister of René de Chateaubriand. This famous explorer had traveled as far as North America, through dense forests to the Appalachian Mountains, Niagara Falls, and the Hudson River. De Chateaubriand wrote books about his travels and about the Indians of North America.

Jules was fascinated by such stories, real and imaginary. He read adventure tales like *Robinson Crusoe* and *The Swiss Family Robinson*. Both books were about island castaways. Jules also read about famous historical events in books by Sir Walter Scott. And he read about the wild, dangerous frontier of North America in *The Leatherstocking Tales* by James Fenimore Cooper.

It was no surprise that Jules's favorite subject in school was geography. But he also did well in mathematics, Latin, and music. Jules was not the best student in his class, but he worked hard and earned good grades.

When he wasn't reading at home or studying in school, Jules explored the Loire River with his brother Paul. They often rented small, leaky boats. In their imaginations, the boats turned into great sailing ships. Sometimes Jules and Paul would beach the boats on one of the river's many sandy islands. They spent long afternoons pretending to be island castaways. In their imaginary world, Jules and his brother built shelters out of driftwood and reeds, foraged for coconuts, and fished for sharks and dolphins.

Just before Jules turned ten years old, his family bought a summer home in Chantenay, a town near Nantes. One summer, Jules rented a small sailboat.

11

He had decided to take a journey down the Loire by himself for the day. He cast off from Chantenay and drifted downstream. When Jules had nearly reached the mouth of the Loire and the sea, his boat struck a rock. One of its planks gave way, and the boat filled with water. Jules had to swim for a small island.

Without his boat he was stranded, just like Robinson Crusoe! He would have to build a shelter and a fire, and find food. What would happen if he was trapped on this island forever? How would he survive?

Jules did not have to wait long for a solution to his problem. After just a few hours, the tide went out, and he discovered an easy escape. The island was connected to the mainland by a strip of sandy beach—he merely had to walk to safety. He was home in time for dinner.

2

Journey to the Center of Paris

In 1845 when he was seventeen years old, Jules Verne began his last year of high school. Pierre Verne expected his son to pass his school exams and begin to study law. But Jules was thinking of other things. Lately he had taken up another interest—writing. He found scribbling in his notebooks much more entertaining than studying. He had already filled four notebooks with a novel, which he called *A Priest in 1839*.

In the spring of 1846, Jules passed his examinations and earned a diploma. He agreed to continue studying and preparing for the exams that would allow him to work as a lawyer. As soon as he finished, he would join his father in business. Pierre planned to rename his firm Verne and Verne.

As a law student, Jules studied legal terms and procedures, and legal writing, research, and speech. But he didn't spend all of his time reading law books. He wrote many poems and scribbled more stories in his notebooks. Just for fun, he also wrote a short play in verse. He sent the play to the Théâtre Riquiqui, a puppet theater. But the theater rejected it.

Jules dedicated many of his poems to his cousin Caroline Tronson. He had fallen in love with his beautiful cousin. He sent her small presents, and he enjoyed talking to her when they met at family dinners or at dancing parties. But Jules was two years younger than Caroline, and she showed little interest in him. In the spring of 1847, she was engaged to another man.

It seemed that most of the families of Nantes did not consider Jules a good match for their daughters. They wanted husbands of property, with high standing in society. A young law student who wrote poetry, even if he was an honest Verne, did not seem suitable.

Jules began to feel restless. Deep down, he wanted to do something great, something people would notice. He didn't want a humdrum career, and he didn't want to stay in a small city like Nantes.

His brother Paul was signing up to be a sailor on a merchant ship. Jules decided to set out for adventure and excitement on land. He asked his father for permission to visit Paris, France's capital. He could stay there with his aunt for several weeks. Pierre Verne agreed to his son's request. In April 1847, the same month as Caroline's wedding, Jules boarded a stagecoach for Tours, another city on the Loire. From Tours, a train took him to Paris.

For a young student from Nantes, Paris looked like the center of the world. The streets were bustling with pedestrians and horse-drawn carriages. There were museums, restaurants, and bookshops. Bankers and stockbrokers worked in fine offices, and businessmen rushed to their appointments. One of the biggest businesses in Paris was entertainment. The theaters of the city drew great crowds to see the finest actors perform in comedies, tragedies, and operas.

France's great capital seemed full of excitement and opportunities. Here Jules was free to do as he liked, without worrying about his father's watchful eye. When Jules returned to Nantes, he convinced Pierre to let him finish his law studies in Paris.

In November 1848, Jules left Nantes once again. He moved into an apartment in the Latin Quarter of Paris. Many students lived in this section of the city.

16

They rented small rooms on the top floors or in the attics of tall stone buildings. They had little money to spend, and to get around town, they walked. Most could only afford simple meals and one or two suits of clothes. Like Jules, they depended on a regular allowance sent by their parents.

Jules's father expected him to pass his final law exam in Paris. But first Jules would have to study and memorize many facts and rules. He quickly learned that studying in Paris was no more interesting than studying in Nantes. He again became bored with his heavy law books. The city and its people inspired him to write plays instead. He began to set down new ideas in his notebooks and write out scenes and the dialogue of imaginary characters. Jules knew that theater managers needed new plays. Perhaps someone would produce one of his plays and make him famous.

At plays and in the homes of friends, Jules met actors, writers, and musicians. One evening, Jules met Alexandre Dumas, one of the most famous authors in the world. His novel *The Three Musketeers* described the adventures of three daring swordsmen in the seventeenth century. The novel captured the imagination of readers in France and all over Europe. It also made Dumas wealthy enough to purchase his own theater, the Théâtre Historique. The theater housed a huge stage that faced five tall tiers of seats. There was room in the theater for more than two thousand spectators.

Jules also made friends with the son of Alexandre Dumas, who was named Alexandre, too. Father and son took an interest in young Jules and his plays. Jules hoped they might help him get one of his plays produced in a theater.

Jules decided to show a short play called *Broken Straws* to the younger Dumas. *Broken Straws* was a comedy about a jealous husband and his flirtatious wife. Dumas read the play and made a few suggestions on how to improve the story. The two friends worked together on *Broken Straws,* then the elder Dumas agreed to put on the play at the Théâtre Historique. Jules would finally see one of his own works on the stage.

The first performance of *Broken Straws* took place in June 1850. The play had a short run of only twelve performances. Later that year, a theater in Nantes also staged *Broken Straws.* Jules's play earned some notice from friends and family, but the ticket sales earned very little money. Jules didn't give up. He would keep writing and earn what Dumas already had—success.

In his letters home, Jules couldn't help expressing

his excitement about the literary world of Paris. But Pierre Verne was not excited or impressed. How could Jules manage to study law properly when he was spending so much time writing plays and meeting writers? Jules reassured his father that his studies always came first. He promised to pass his exam.

Jules kept a part of his promise. By the end of 1850, he had managed to pass his final law exam. He knew that his father was waiting for him to come home. He also knew that he could not leave Paris. If he moved back to Nantes, Paris would soon forget all about him and his plays.

In the spring of 1851, Jules wrote a long letter to his father that explained everything. "Literature means more to me than anything else," he wrote, "because that is all I can succeed at." He explained that he wouldn't make a very good lawyer, because "I only see the comic or artistic aspect of things."

When he read the letter, Pierre Verne felt anger and disappointment at his son's foolish whim. Pierre didn't believe that writing was a serious career, and he was sure that Jules would not succeed. He wanted his son to come home to Nantes and get to work. But Jules was stubborn, and Pierre agreed to lend him money for a while. With the money, Jules could rent an apartment and buy some furniture. He could also earn money as a law clerk and as a tutor for law students in Paris.

Jules wanted to see his plays succeed. He also would prove to his father that he could make a living as a writer. To earn money, Jules started writing for a magazine called the *Musée des Familles*. The magazine published articles on history, geography, religion, and travel. It also ran fictional stories about the wide world outside the borders of France.

Jules came up with ideas for the magazine from his reading and researching. He enjoyed finding information almost as much as writing. Jules passed many mornings at the Bibliothèque Nationale, the national library. The library owned nearly every book printed in France. Thousands of books about geography, history, science, mathematics, and philosophy were gathered on miles of wooden shelves.

The library didn't allow anyone to borrow its books. Jules had to study them at small reading desks inside the library. He also read magazine and newspaper articles to keep up with the latest events. In small notebooks and on note cards, he wrote down every single fact that interested him. He soon had dozens of files filled with facts. He memorized numbers, dates, places, events, and names.

Geography was still one of Jules's favorite topics.

As a child, he had read adventure tales that took him all over the world. In a geography book, he could visit distant countries and imagine amazing sights. He could also read about the places people hoped to someday explore. Nobody had yet invented a ship to visit the deep ocean floor. The top of the world's highest mountain, Mount Everest, was unseen by humans. Explorers had not reached the distant North Pole. And Europeans had yet to discover the source of the Nile River in Africa, the longest river in the world.

In his search for facts, Jules also sought out explorers. A friend introduced him to Jacques Arago. This famous adventurer had been to the far corners of the world. He had described many of his travels in a popular book called *Voyage Around the World.*

Jacques Arago and Jules became good friends. The explorer inspired Jules with his descriptions of the world. He had seen the Antarctic continent, the rain forests and deserts of Asia, and the rivers of South America. He had even searched for gold in the mountains of Colorado and California. Through Jacques and books, Jules discovered a world much bigger and more interesting than Paris.

By the summer of 1851, Jules had completed his first story for the *Musée des Familles.* The story's title was "The First Ships of the Mexican Navy." It described a mutiny on board a Spanish ship. The adventure took place in the Pacific Ocean, California, and Mexico.

Jules roamed far in his story. But he had never traveled outside France. Just like his favorite authors, he had used his powerful imagination to take himself on great adventures.

3

Husband and Businessman

In 1852 Jules began working for the Théâtre Lyrique, which had changed its name from the Théâtre Historique. He spent long days in the theater and watched its plays at night. He saw several of his stories published, and his plays had been produced on the stages of Paris. But nothing he wrote had yet made the name of Jules Verne famous.

Jules was beginning to grow tired of his busy life in Paris. His witty friends were telling the same jokes over and over. Famous people he met seemed ordinary. The latest plays grew boring, and good restaurants grew stale. Jules enjoyed his freedom in Paris, but he also began to feel lonely. Many of his friends were getting married, and Jules had been attending weddings large and small. Perhaps it was time for him to marry and settle down, too.

In the spring of 1856, his friend Auguste Lelarge invited Jules to his wedding. It took place in the town of Amiens in northern France. For a week, Jules danced and talked with other guests and enjoyed himself. He also fell in love.

At the wedding party, Jules met Honorine Deviane, the sister of the bride. Honorine was a widow with two young daughters, Suzanne and Valentine. She was a light-hearted woman, eager to talk and laugh with everyone. She was good-natured and very practical, and Jules thought she would make a fine wife.

Over the next few weeks, Jules wrote enthusiastic letters about Honorine to his parents. He was falling in love with her, but he was being practical as well. Honorine's family, he wrote, could help him become a businessman. That summer, Jules asked Mr. Deviane, Honorine's father, for his daughter's hand in marriage.

To support his future wife, Jules would learn how to become a businessman from Honorine's brother.

Ferdinand Deviane worked as a stockbroker in Amiens. For his customers, he bought and sold stock in different companies. Owning a company's stocks was like owning a small part or share of a company. A stockbroker hoped the stocks would go up in value so that he and his customers could make a profit.

Ferdinand promised to help Jules become a stockbroker. The work was easy, and Jules wouldn't need years of study. His chance would come at a stockbrokerage in Paris called Eggly & Co. After Ferdinand told him about Eggly & Co., Jules wrote to his father to ask for a very important favor. If Pierre Verne could lend him some money to buy a share in this firm, Jules could become a partner. He could finally settle down, marry Honorine, and perhaps raise a family. He would write in his spare time.

By this time, Pierre Verne realized that his son would never become a lawyer in Nantes. There would be no law firm of Verne and Verne. He wasn't sure that Jules could be a stockbroker, either. Jules didn't seem like a businessman of any kind. Yet Pierre wanted to see his son try a serious career. He agreed to help Jules invest in Eggly & Co.

On January 10, 1857, Jules and Honorine were officially married in a Paris city office and then at a simple ceremony in the church of St. Eugene. After the wedding, they moved into a new apartment in Paris. Honorine's two daughters—Jules's new stepchildren—stayed temporarily in Amiens with their father's parents.

Jules settled into an entirely new life. Every morning, he walked from his apartment to the offices of Eggly & Co. He spent many afternoons at the Bourse, the big stock exchange in the center of Paris. Here hundreds of stockbrokers worked at their desks, buying and selling stocks to make a profit.

Jules watched the other brokers carefully. He soon learned the tricks of buying and selling stocks and making money. He read newspapers carefully, trying to predict how events in the world would affect prices. Like everyone else, he tried to buy the stocks cheap and sell them when their value rose. Sometimes he succeeded, and sometimes he failed, but he did manage to make a living.

Jules felt proud of the change in his life. It seemed that his father finally supported a choice he had made. But after a few months, he also found that he cared little for his job. Instead of trading stocks, he preferred reading books and newspapers, or just chatting with other brokers. Instead of making bids, he talked about the latest plays and news and gossiped with his friends at the Bourse. His thoughts were turning once more to writing. He realized that he would rather make his fortune by writing, and he still believed that he could.

In 1859 Jules's friend Aristide Hignard called on him with exciting news. Hignard's father, who was a shipping agent, had two tickets for a steamship bound for Scotland. The ship would stop at several ports and sail across the North Sea to the British Isles. For the first time in his life, Jules would leave France. He eagerly took this chance to leave work behind for a while.

The two friends sailed to Edinburgh, Scotland. They took trains and carriages through England and finally reached London. During the trip, Jules took many pages of notes. This real adventure would supply him with new ideas for his writing. He wrote down his schedules and a list of the cities he saw. He described places and people. He also wrote long letters home telling about the journey. Jules was especially impressed by a gigantic unfinished steamship he saw in London. The *Great Eastern* would make voyages across the Atlantic Ocean and around the world. When finished, it would be the largest ship ever built.

When he returned to France, Jules again took up his career as a stockbroker. He also made his travel notes and memories into a novel. In his novel, he gave himself the name Jacques Laveret. His friend Hignard became Jonathan Savournan. Jules called the book *Voyage en Angleterre et en Ecosse* (A Journey to England and Scotland).

Jules sent the book to several different publishers. None were interested in his *Voyage en Angleterre et en Ecosse.* Book publishers didn't believe people wanted to read about ordinary travel. Instead, they wanted adventures of another time and place—books that took them far away from their ordinary lives. They wanted stories with dashing heroes, like *The Three Musketeers,* or tales of danger in exotic places, like *The Leatherstocking Tales.*

Jules hardly had time to be discouraged. In the summer of 1861, he departed for another trip with Aristide. This time they journeyed to Scandinavia. But the trip was cut short by other important events taking place at home. In the early morning of August 5, 1861, Honorine gave birth to a baby boy. Jules and Honorine named him Michel.

Jules was proud to have a healthy son, but he soon had trouble with young Michel. While Jules worked in his study, the baby cried, screamed, and whimpered in the next room. Michel often made it hard to write, talk, read, or even think. Many times, Jules lost patience and flew into rages. Honorine cared for the baby as best she could. It was not easy living with a husband who needed so much quiet time to write.

Jules pressed on. A new idea had taken hold of him. He wanted to write a story that would take place in distant Africa, a continent that fascinated many people. Much of Africa was still unknown to Europeans, and very few of them had ever set foot there. Jules had never been to Africa. But he had read about it, and he could imagine one exciting way to travel there—riding the air currents in a hot air balloon.

Passenger balloons had existed for nearly one hundred years. The first were built and flown by daring inventors who risked their lives flying high over the countryside of France. While working on his balloon story, Jules met one of these daring balloonists. Felix Tournachon, also known as Nadar, was building his own hot air balloon called the *Géant* (Giant). Hot air balloons like the *Géant* had captured the public's imagination. Like Jules, people dreamed of leaving the ground and flying through the air from place to place.

Jules used the research he had done on balloons and Africa to write his new adventure. It told the story of a daring scientist named Dr. Ferguson who flies across Africa in a balloon called the *Victoria*. Using heated gas, Ferguson can raise and lower the *Victoria* to catch the winds.

Jules carefully explained the balloon's construction. He also described the African deserts and rain forests. He was creating a new kind of novel, mixing geographical facts and scientific discoveries with an exciting fictional story.

In the summer of 1862, Jules finished his book. He brought the manuscript to François Buloz, who published a popular magazine called the *Revue des Deux Mondes*. After reading Jules's book, Buloz offered to print the story in the *Revue*. But he wouldn't pay anything for it. After all, Buloz said, his readers had never heard of Jules Verne.

Jules couldn't afford to publish his novel without pay. He turned down the offer and continued to search for a publisher. One day in the early autumn of 1862, he brought his manuscript to the offices of Hetzel & Compagnie, on the Rue Jacob in Paris. Jules had heard that this publisher was looking for good stories. And he knew he had a good story.

4

Meeting Monsieur Hetzel

Jules Hetzel's office on the Rue Jacob held hundreds of thick, handwritten manuscripts from all over France. Many of them came from writers like Jules Verne, unknown and ambitious. Others came from famous writers like Honoré de Balzac and George Sand.

Hetzel spent hours reading these manuscripts. He rejected most of them. There were so many writers, but so few of them knew how to please the public! Didn't they realize that readers wanted a good story with believable characters? The characters must do interesting things, and they must speak and act in a realistic way. They must take part in a dramatic, suspenseful story that has a satisfying ending. It seemed that very few writers could do all of this and make it seem easy.

Jules Verne's manuscript stood out from all the rest.

It had many of the elements needed for a good book. Hetzel decided to give this new writer a chance. Indeed, he might publish this novel about an adventurous balloon flight. Hot air balloons were very popular in France. If Jules would carefully rewrite according to his instructions, Hetzel believed the book would appeal to many readers.

Jules was thrilled to find a publisher for his book. He set to work on it immediately, changing sentences and replacing paragraphs. He scribbled down new scenes and dialogue in tiny handwriting that he squeezed between the lines. He worked day and night, while Michel cried and Honorine grew exasperated. Finally he returned to Hetzel's office with the new and improved story. Hetzel accepted the novel. He decided to publish it as *Five Weeks in a Balloon.*

In meeting Jules Verne, Hetzel realized that he had made an important discovery. Verne had a rare talent. Like Charles Dickens, Edgar Allan Poe, and other popular writers, Jules Verne knew how to keep readers glued to the page. He wrote well enough to satisfy the public's demand for a good tale. He also drew on an entirely new and modern inspiration, the world of science and invention.

The world was changing rapidly. Scientists and inventors were making new discoveries all the time.

Their work allowed people to communicate and travel faster than ever before. Inventors were creating amazing machines such as telegraphs, steam locomotives, and submarines. And geographers were learning astonishing new facts about the earth. Hetzel's readers wanted to know about it all.

Jules Verne knew how to write exciting stories about the rapidly changing world. He also had the ability to explain the possible—what scientists and explorers *might* invent, build, and accomplish in the future. Of all the writers in France, Hetzel realized, only Jules was combining science and fiction in this way.

Hetzel decided to offer Jules a contract to write *three* new books every year. The publisher would pay 1,925 francs for each book! That was more than Jules had lived on for a whole year as a student in Paris. The novels would be part of a new series for young readers called Extraordinary Voyages.

Hetzel had even dreamed up a magazine for this new style of writing. It was to be called the *Magasin d'Education et de Récréation* (Magazine of Learning and Leisure). Hetzel planned to publish each Jules Verne novel in installments. A chapter of the novel would appear in the magazine every two weeks, until the entire novel was printed. After the whole novel was printed in the magazine, Hetzel would also publish it as a regular, hardcover illustrated book.

Five Weeks in a Balloon appeared in late 1862, just before the Christmas holiday. People all over France were searching for Christmas presents for their friends and families. Jules's book sold many thousands of copies. He was delighted to see his first book become a best-seller. After years of writing plays and stories, Jules was finally beginning the career he had dreamed about. He was no longer Jules Verne, average stockbroker. At the age of thirty-four, he had become Jules Verne, famous author.

Many people took *Five Weeks in a Balloon* for a true account of real events. Like the book's hero, Dr. Ferguson, real explorers were reaching the unknown parts of Africa. While Jules had been working on *Five Weeks in a Balloon,* James Grant and John Speke had been searching for the source of the Nile River. They finally found it during the summer of 1862, just as Jules was finishing his own African adventure.

After Jules's novel appeared, Nadar finished work on his balloon the *Géant.* Newspapers and magazines wrote about the great event. Photographs and illustrations appeared on their front pages.

In the summer of 1863, Nadar and his assistants prepared the *Géant* for its first flight. Nadar's workers brought the hot air balloon to a grassy, open field.

After the anchor ropes of the *Géant* were untied, the balloon lifted slowly from the ground. A breeze caught the balloon and carried it over the rooftops of Paris. A few hours later, it came down safely several miles away.

Hundreds of spectators, reporters, and photographers had gathered to witness the event. Many of them had read *Five Weeks in a Balloon.* It seemed that the flight Jules had described in his book had just come true with the flight of Nadar's *Géant.*

5

A Successful Author

With *Five Weeks in a Balloon,* Jules had attracted a loyal audience. Excited readers made the hard work of writing much easier and more fun. In fact, Jules had already begun working on another book, a sea adventure. In this novel, Jules introduced a character named Captain Hatteras. This rugged explorer sails to the Arctic Ocean to discover a route to the North Pole. It would be forty-five years before explorer Robert Peary would become the first person to reach the North Pole. But Jules's readers could visit this dangerous and faraway destination in his book.

In March 1864, Hetzel published the beginning of *The Adventures of Captain Hatteras* in the first issue of his new magazine. The novel became the first in the Extraordinary Voyages series. It was also the first of many stories about the popular Captain Hatteras, who would journey all over the world.

At home, Jules wrote every day, using his notes, pen, paper, and imagination. It was like traveling with his mind. He could go everywhere and describe everything he saw. When he finished one book, he immediately started another. He sometimes had two, three, or more unfinished books going at once. Jules filled thick notebooks with ideas, notes, dialogue, and scenes for new stories.

Once he finished a book, Jules turned the manuscript over to his publisher. Hetzel wrote corrections and suggestions on the sides or the tops of the pages. He suggested new twists in the plot or ways to improve the story. Then he sent the book back to Jules. Jules made his changes, and the two men traded the manuscript back and forth several more times. Finally, when both were satisfied, the book was published.

As readers followed Captain Hatteras on his adventures, Jules was discovering an idea for another book. He had been reading the work of an American named

John Symmes. Symmes believed that long passageways existed inside the earth. By finding and following them, Symmes explained, an explorer might make his way to the center of the planet. The idea of such an expedition intrigued Jules.

In *A Journey to the Center of the Earth,* Jules explained how someone might make this kind of exploration using the latest inventions. Jules supplied his characters with a new kind of lantern that a scientist in Paris had recently invented. Made of a copper wire coil, the lantern used an experimental energy force called electricity. In Jules's story, the electric coil lights the way for the explorers as they discover caves and tunnels inside the earth. Jules introduced his readers to this electric lantern fifteen years before Thomas Edison's electric light bulb ushered in the age of electricity.

In his mind's eye, Jules saw many things that people might invent and do in the future. The more he wrote, the more he imagined great adventures and fantastic inventions. He even began to think about an adventure in outer space. Since the first balloon flight, astronomers had wondered if space travel was possible. But no one had discovered a practical way to reach outer space.

By reading articles about the American Civil War,

Jules learned that armies were using terrifying modern machinery. Big guns could throw a cannonball many miles. Perhaps similar machinery could launch a rocket to the Moon.

In his next book, *From the Earth to the Moon,* Jules dreamed up a spaceship that travels to the Moon. He made the spaceship large enough to hold three men and two dogs. It was made out of aluminum, one of the lightest metals. It was also stocked with water, food, and air. Jules created an air-supply system for his fictional astronauts, since he knew that outer space has no atmosphere. And in his novel, the aluminum rocket was launched from the coast of Florida, close to Earth's equator.

To Jules's readers, *From the Earth to the Moon* was just a fantasy. Travel to the Moon seemed like a preposterous idea! It wasn't until the 1960s, nearly one hundred years after Jules wrote his novel, that the first rockets were launched to the Moon. Like Jules's fictional invention, they were made with aluminum, had an air-supply system, and were launched from the coast of Florida.

For a writer who explored as far as the Moon in his imagination, Jules did not travel much. He usually stayed at home, traveling only in his books. In Paris, he could spend all day inside a library or a museum.

He filled his head with facts and useful details that would later appear in a story. It was easy for him to visit Hetzel, who provided help and inspiration for his books. He also paid calls on friends and writers who lived in the city.

Still, Paris was a crowded, hectic, and noisy place. In the small apartment where he lived with his wife, son, and two stepdaughters, Jules could not find the quiet he needed to work. His young son was proving to be a difficult child who sometimes distracted Jules from his writing.

In the spring of 1866, Jules decided to move away from Paris with his family. The Vernes settled in Le Crotoy, a small fishing village on the English Channel, not far from Amiens. Le Crotoy could be a cold, rainy, cloudy, and gloomy place. But Jules loved the sights and smells of the sea. He liked rough seas and rainy weather as much as a crowded theater or a library's bookshelf. He spent many afternoons walking along the harbor, watching the fishing boats, cargo ships, and yachts pass by. Not long after moving to Le Crotoy, he bought his own boat and named it the *Saint Michel,* after his son. Jules could spend weeks on his boat, sailing along the coasts of northern France with his family or on his own.

The sea seemed endless. It was a world where a

small boat like the *Saint Michel* could be lost forever. And underneath the sea was an unknown world that explorers had yet to discover. Jules knew that this world must hold many astounding landscapes and creatures of its own. He began writing a book about just such an adventure.

In March 1867, Jules and his brother Paul journeyed to New York on the *Great Eastern*. Jules had seen this enormous steamship years before while visiting London with his friend Aristide Hignard. After arriving in New York, he and his brother had several days to explore the big city. They also visited Niagara Falls and saw the Erie Canal. Everywhere they went, Jules stored away new ideas.

When he returned to France, Jules was anxious to return to his latest adventure, an undersea voyage in a submarine. Jules had read about submarines built in France, and he knew they had been used during the American Civil War. These submarines could spend hours underwater, spying on enemy ships while roaming beneath the waves. But they could not go very deep, or the tremendous pressure of the water would destroy them. They were also very small, only big enough for a single submariner.

In Jules's submarine adventure, a man named Professor Aronnax discovers that a frightening sea monster is actually a giant submarine known as the *Nautilus*. The skipper of this strange craft is the mysterious Captain Nemo. Nemo explains that the ship runs on an amazing energy source: "There is a powerful agent, obedient, rapid, easy, which conforms to every use. . . .Everything is done by means of it. . . .This agent is electricity."

Professor Aronnax also learns that Nemo's submarine has its own air-supply system. The ship can stay underwater for days at a time without running out of air. Its thick steel body resists the crushing pressure of the ocean depths. The powerful *Nautilus* can even survive a journey under the frozen South Pole.

Jules called his submarine novel *Twenty Thousand Leagues Under the Sea*. When it appeared in 1870, Verne and Hetzel had another wildly successful book. Readers all over France enjoyed the exciting story of the mysterious Captain Nemo and his amazing deep-sea submarine. Little did they know that Jules had predicted the future of submarines! In about eighty years, modern submarines would have their own self-contained air supply, and many would be made of steel. With a new source of energy—nuclear power—they would be able to remain underwater for weeks and months. In fact, the first nuclear-powered submarine would be named the *Nautilus*.

But when Jules was writing, stories like *Twenty Thousand Leagues Under the Sea* seemed to be just an entertaining guess at the future. They were ideas by an author with a wild imagination.

6

Famous Around the World

Jules had little time to enjoy the great success of *Twenty Thousand Leagues Under the Sea.* In 1870, a war broke out between France and its powerful neighbor, Prussia. Jules moved his family to Amiens, Honorine's hometown. He believed they would be safer in Amiens than along the coast, where he thought Prussian ships might attack. Jules stayed in Le Crotoy to help patrol the coastal beaches. He placed a small cannon on the front of the *Saint Michel.* He brought the boat out into the bay and watched for enemy ships.

The war went badly for France. The French emperor, Napoleon III, fell from power, and a new government ruled the country. The people of France wanted to forget the hardships of war by reading more stories of adventure in distant lands. Most of them already knew the name of Jules Verne. At the age of forty-three, he had won over readers of all ages.

In 1871 Hetzel decided it was time to offer Jules a new contract. Instead of three books a year, he asked for only two. He would pay six thousand francs for each new book—three times what he had paid Jules for *Five Weeks in a Balloon.*

Jules was anxious to get back to his writing desk. In the summer of 1871, he joined his family in Amiens. Honorine's hometown was a small city, much smaller than Paris, but livelier than little Le Crotoy. It seemed like a good place to settle down. In Amiens, Jules could work on his stories in peace and still find time to sail his boat or enjoy the company of friends and family.

After he moved to Amiens, Jules began working on a new travel adventure. He remembered when most people used their feet or their horses to travel from place to place. When he was a boy, it took a long time to travel to a neighboring country and even longer to voyage to another continent. Few people traveled long distances. Only a *very* few went all the way around the world. By sailing ship, the only possible way, it could take a year or longer to circle the globe. But with modern steamships and railroads, traveling had become much quicker. Jules thought of the speedy *Great Eastern* and the fast-moving trains he had seen in the United States.

Jules's new novel was about an Englishman named Phileas Fogg. Mr. Fogg appears to be a very ordinary man. His schedule is always the same, day after day. And he always arrives on time, no matter where he is going.

One day, Mr. Fogg makes a very risky bet. He believes it is possible to travel around the world in eighty days, and he bets his friends twenty thousand pounds that he can do it himself. Using the most modern forms of transportation, Mr. Fogg starts out on his worldwide adventure with his servant Passepartout (whose name means "goes everywhere"). The two men cross the English Channel, ride the trains through Europe, and board a steamboat to the Suez Canal. They travel through India, Hong Kong, Japan, and the United States. Finally they return safely to England with only seconds to spare. Phileas Fogg travels the world in exactly eighty days and wins his bet.

Around the World in Eighty Days appeared in the newspaper *Le Temps* in 1873. At the same time, it was sold as a hardcover book. It turned out to be the most popular novel Jules had ever written. Nearly a half-million copies were sold during his lifetime. The book made Jules Verne famous around the world.

By 1875 Jules Hetzel was earning more money from Jules Verne than from any other author. Since he first brought out *Five Weeks in a Balloon,* Hetzel had been publishing two or three new Verne books every year. The books always sold well, especially in the weeks before Christmas. Parents all over France bought them as presents for their children. His books had also been translated into many other languages. Jules Verne had loyal readers in Germany, Russia, Italy, Spain, England, and the United States. In the 1870s, three different British publishers were printing Jules's books in English. In 1876 alone, seventeen new Verne titles appeared in England.

Verne had been loyal to Hetzel. It was time for Hetzel to return Jules's loyalty. Instead of a yearly fee, he would pay Jules a royalty. This was a payment for each book that was sold. Because there were so many of his books in print, and because they sold so well, the royalties would make Jules a wealthy man.

With the money he was earning, Jules decided to buy a new boat. The *Saint Michel III* was ninety-two feet long and powered by a steam engine. In order to sail the *Saint Michel III,* Jules had to hire a captain and a crew. With this boat, he could travel anywhere in the world in comfort. He could also leave behind reporters and fans for a while.

Jules took many long voyages aboard the *Saint Michel III.* Sometimes he cruised with friends, other times with family. He invited his brother Paul and his nephew Gaston aboard. Gaston was Paul's son and one of Jules's favorite nephews. Jules also brought his son Michel on his travels.

In 1884 Jules took his family on a voyage to the Mediterranean Sea. He had the clouds and ocean for company, while the crowds and noise of France remained far away. In the privacy of his small cabin, he could read and write and not be interrupted. But when he ordered his ship into a port, he found that it was hard to keep his privacy. No matter where he went, his books had arrived before him.

Everywhere he went, people greeted him and congratulated him for his famous stories. In Tunisia the Vernes enjoyed a grand banquet given by the king. In Rome the pope invited Jules to his office for a private meeting. In Venice the people of the city held a great celebration that ended with a spectacular fireworks display.

Everyone, it seemed, had read books by Jules Verne. All enjoyed his strange and exciting adventures in faraway places. Plays based on his stories filled theaters in Paris and in other cities. His name was known all over the world. And his visions of amazing inventions and daring explorations had captured the imaginations of millions of readers.

Afterword

After the success of *Twenty Thousand Leagues Under the Sea* and *Around the World in Eighty Days,* Jules became very famous. Reporters visited his home hoping to interview the popular author, and his new books continued to sell. Jules tried as hard as he could to lead a quiet life. He spent his days writing, visiting friends, and going to social clubs in Amiens.

Then on March 9, 1886, tragedy touched his life. On that day, Jules was returning to his house in the afternoon. As he reached the front gate, his nephew Gaston suddenly rushed up to him. Gaston was suffering from a mental illness. Terrible visions and nightmares came to him, making him frightened of almost everything and everyone. He had taken a train to Amiens to find his uncle.

When Gaston saw Jules at his front door, he pulled out a gun and fired. Gaston missed his uncle by only a few inches. He pulled the trigger again and ran away. The second bullet struck Jules in the foot near his ankle. The foot was badly hurt and didn't heal completely. Jules walked with a limp. He could no longer move around or travel or sail as he had. Many days, he could not leave his house at all. He stayed at his desk or in a reading chair. He drew away from many of his friends and members of his family.

One way to fight his troubles was to continue working as hard as he could. With the help of secretaries who took down his stories as he told them, he finished new books every year. In these later books, Jules wrote about motion pictures, helicopters, televisions, and skyscrapers—none of which had yet been invented.

On March 24, 1905, Jules quietly died in his bed at the age of seventy-seven. A few days later, he was buried in a cemetery in Amiens. A sculpture placed over his resting place read "Onward to Immortality and Eternal Youth."

During his lifetime, Jules Verne published more than sixty-five novels. His tales of adventure had influenced countless people. Scientists and inventors who grew up reading Jules Verne's stories were making remarkable discoveries. Many of the predictions

Jules had made in his books were coming true.

People continued to read Jules Verne's novels, and popular movies were made from them. The movie versions of *Around the World in Eighty Days* and *Twenty Thousand Leagues Under the Sea* played to large audiences all over the world.

Some people call Jules Verne the creator of science fiction. Jules may have been the first to use actual scientific theories and discoveries in his stories. But his books are not simply about science. Jules Verne's books are adventures of the human heart and soul.

Selected Works by Jules Verne*

Books

1863 *Five Weeks in a Balloon*
1864 *A Journey to the Center of the Earth*
1865 *From the Earth to the Moon*
1867 *The Adventures of Captain Hatteras*
1869 *Twenty Thousand Leagues Under the Sea*
1870 *Around the Moon*
1873 *Around the World in Eighty Days*
1874 *The Mysterious Island*
1876 *Michael Strogoff*
1877 *Hector Servadac*
1886 *Robur the Conqueror*
1892 *The Castle in the Carpathians*
1904 *Master of the World*

* Dates given are for the original French publication

Bibliography

Born, Franz. *Jules Verne: The Man Who Invented the Future.* Englewood Cliffs, NJ: Prentice-Hall, 1964.

Costello, Peter. *Jules Verne: Inventor of Science Fiction.* New York: Charles Scribner's Sons, 1978.

Freedman, Russell. *Jules Verne: Portrait of a Prophet.* New York: Holiday House, 1965.

Jules-Verne, Jean. *Jules Verne.* New York: Taplinger Publishing Company, 1976.

Lottman, Herbert R. *Jules Verne: An Exploratory Biography.* New York: St. Martin's Press, 1996.

Taves, Brian and Stephen Michaluk, Jr. *The Jules Verne Encyclopedia.* London: Scarecrow Press, Inc., 1996.

Verne, Jules. *Twenty Thousand Leagues Under the Sea.* New York: The Heritage Press, 1956.

Index

About the Author

Tom Streissguth has spent several years in France among friends and relations. He also helps to organize and operate a summer language school that takes place in northern France. During his visits to the country, Mr. Streissguth has traveled "in all kinds of newfangled contraptions," including high-speed trains and Citroën cars. When he is not undertaking such Vernelike adventures, Mr. Streissguth enjoys reading novels by Jules Verne and other French authors. He has written many books for children, including several biographies for Carolrhoda Books. Mr. Streissguth and his wife make their home in Sarasota, Florida.

About the Illustrator

Ralph L. Ramstad has been drawing pictures "since the age of three." Like Jules Verne, he enjoys combining research with creative work. "Histories and biographies, particularly of the eighteenth and nineteenth centuries. . . . are my great favorites." Mr. Ramstad studied at the Pratt Institute in Brooklyn, New York. For forty-two years, he created art for product packaging, print advertisements, and billboards. He has also illustrated several biographies and histories for Carolrhoda Books. Mr. Ramstad lives with his wife in Minneapolis, Minnesota.